THE WILD DELIGHT OF WILD THINGS

BRIAN TURNER

THE
DELI
OF
THI

ALICE JAMES BOOKS
New Gloucester, ME
alicejamesbooks.org

CELEBRATING 50 YEARS
OF ALICE JAMES BOOKS

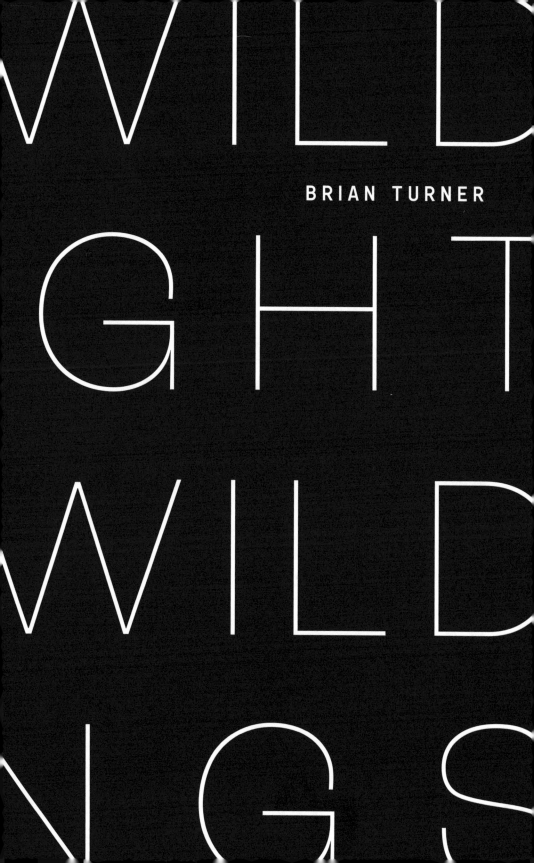

WILD LIGHT WILD THINGS

BRIAN TURNER

10 9 8 7 6 5 4 3 2 1

Alice James Books are published by Alice James Poetry Cooperative, Inc.

Alice James Books

Auburn Hall

60 Pineland Drive, Suite 206

New Gloucester, ME 04260

www.alicejamesbooks.org

Library of Congress Cataloging-in-Publication Data

Names: Turner, Brian, 1967–
Title: The wild delight of wild things / Brian Turner.
Description: New Gloucester, ME : Alice James Books, 2023.
Identifiers: LCCN 2023001690 (print) | LCCN 2023001691 (ebook)
    ISBN 9781949944532 (trade paperback) | ISBN 9781949944266 (ebook)
Subjects: LCGFT: Poetry.
Classification: LCC PS3620.U763 W55 2023 (print) | LCC PS3620.U763 (ebook)
    DDC 811/.6—dc23/eng/20230410
LC record available at https://lccn.loc.gov/2023001690
LC ebook record available at https://lccn.loc.gov/2023001691

Alice James Books gratefully acknowledges support from individual donors, private foundations, the National Endowment for the Arts, and the Amazon Literary Partnership.

Cover Photo: "51. Japanese Sea Nettles" from *More Than Human* by Tim Flach *for Ilyse*

CONTENTS

GEOLOGIC

When I don't have a body anymore. When
I'm ash and fragmented bone. I think about
the early people, trapped between one

geological era and another, unfathomable.
Their dust must yearn to rise but can't.
So much pressure on their carbon, hydrogen,

trace elements we've lost, forgotten.
Will we all become diamonds? Will anything of us
beyond an uncertain glimmer survive?

Remember when we visited the animal refuge,
fed parakeets in the aviary from ice-cream sticks
glittering with seeds? The tickle and nudge

of their beaks, a perfect engulfment—
the wild delight of wild things, my love,
I hope we'll have that again.

—*Ilyse Kusnetz*

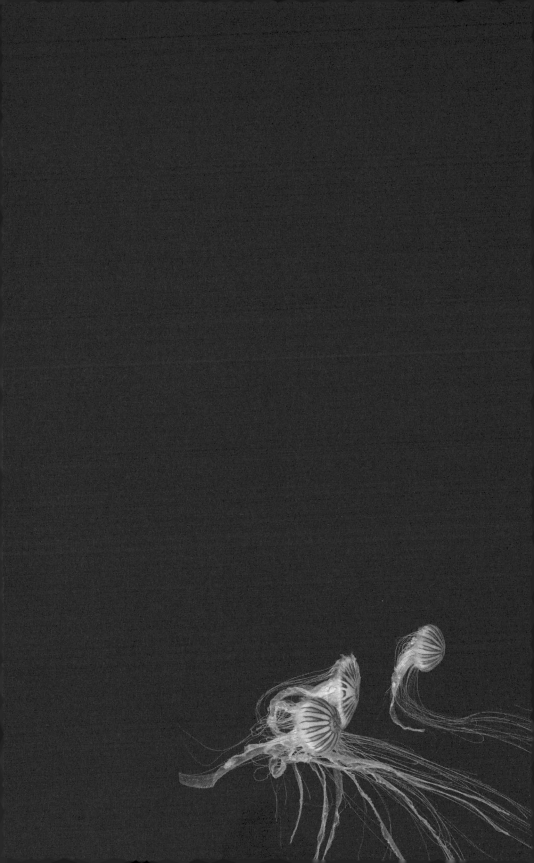

ANNA MARIA ISLAND

Did you know that each wave—like the one curling ashore with an acoustic boom that flattens into a wash of foam—is an expression of the invisible? It's true. Waves are not made of water. They travel through it. And while some waves are tidal in nature, dependent on the forces of gravity, many are driven by sunlight, strange as that might sound. They are the result of wind over water, wind generated through inversions of heat and cold. So much of it determined by the sun.

Barefoot, I head into the surf, bracing myself as each wave washes past, moving forward in the periods between, the sand at my feet trying to suck me down into the earth as I press on until I'm far enough out that the ocean floor sinks away and the water lifts me into its fluid suspension—weightless and free. Seagulls wheel and turn in an aerial geometry. I dunk my head under to soak my hair, cool and slick, the taste of salt on my tongue.

The water around me has a milky-green glow to it, nearly phosphorescent in the morning sun, and there's something essential I can feel but don't yet have the language to name.

There's so much I don't understand. Like the stillness in our home. The urn with your ashes in the bedroom, the way the carved wooden Buddha never shifts its gaze while watching over you. That cool feel of you beside me in bed, late at night, as the planet spins on, the way it does, as if nothing has changed. As if you didn't die in my arms. As if I didn't hold you as you breathed the spirit out of your body. That last breath.

The arrival of a wave is similar to the arrival of an inevitable idea, though the source of it began some time ago, far from here, in a moment that now feels disconnected and final. Perhaps this is why I sometimes sense the eternal as my body drifts in the ocean. Like the ocean, the fluid medium of our minds, that space of fire and electricity and memory, is comprised mostly of water and salt. I'm reminded of new advances in the field of neuroscience, which has shifted from the use of exterior electrodes in electroencephalograms to the direct application of sensors on the surface of the human brain in electrocorticography. The current research suggests, as Simon Makin states in *Scientific American*, that "many brain waves are actually 'traveling waves' that physically move through the brain like waves on the sea."

We are tiny oceans that have learned how to speak with one another. And to carry each other in memory. To carry all that has vanished from the turning of the Earth.

I'm thinking of your laughter. The bright roll of it filling the air. Your hand in mine as we walked the shoreline and talked about the future. I remember you saying that our species has a kind of nostalgia for the future. That there's a sweetness in our wonder. Your hands shaping the air in front of us as you imagined these things, gesturing them into being. We soaked it all in. The island. The beach. The meditation of saltwater and sand submerging our feet.

Snowy plovers evaded the rush of bubbling spume with their thin legs blurring, while the silhouettes of pelicans seemed to freeze stock-still in the amber sky like a series of still-frames over the wavetops. The sun burned its slow signature into the ocean, with shades of lavender and peach feathering the descent—as if it recognized that on any given day on Earth, this would be the only one like it ever to exist. That something as rare as this should end in beauty. A beauty scaled to grandeur. With the two of us given an ocean of dusk to wade into. Twilight. Cicadas trilling the humid air.

It's been almost four years. Time as cruel and as inexorable as the waves, breaking.

I packed the car this morning and drove for hours playing our road-trip music, just as we did summers back. I signed our names in the guest book and took two cookies from the tray. When the manager posed the usual questions, I spoke of us in the present tense. I'm not sure it made a difference. It's not so difficult to witness the subtle ways that death moves through the expressions on my face, that slow cloud of grief that most reel away from, though, here and there, some recognize for the beauty that it is. This carrying of the dead. It felt so good to be honest like that, to be closer to the truth. I didn't repeat the lie that makes you vanish a little more with each telling.

And so here we are—all checked-in to our little love nest by the sea, the two of us wading barefoot into the surf, hand in hand, here to float in the warm waters of the Gulf once more, our troubles fading with each rise and fall, the world a world away as swells of blue-green water roll in, each wave lifting us off our feet and into the cool air, our bodies so buoyant and light, so light we could bring all the midnights and mornings of our lives with us and still the swells would continue to lift us into that vast and cloudless field of blue.

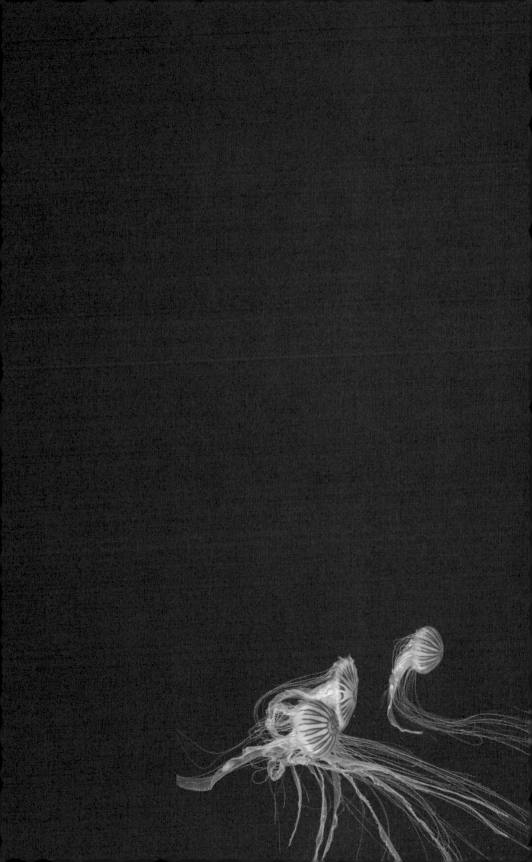

THE IMMORTALS

Bell-shaped and translucent, jellyfish begin their ascent from the ocean floor.
They've completed a novel process in the animal kingdom: transdifferentiation.
It's a reversal of the biological cycle as we know it—undoing the narrative arc
tracing birth to adulthood before the inevitable decline and death. The jellyfish
upend everything we know about death in flora and fauna. At the cellular level,
they grow *younger* when the time comes to die. They transform backwards
into a nascent version of themselves before starting the process over.

It doesn't mean they are incapable of dying—it's simply not in their nature.
They rise through the midnight-dark waters and into bands of sunlight
the way thought forms in the subconscious before burning in waves
across the neocortex of the human brain. And as they rise,
fathom by fathom, they become lighter. As each incarnation
returns, history unfolds and the world is made new. They rise
into the Age of Agriculture with its domestication of wild grain,
with the comprehension of seed to stem to fruit. They witness
the emergence of cities. Wheels and alphabets and metallurgy.
Buddha and Confucius, Jesus and Mohammed. The Age of Flight
and the Age of Information. The jellyfish descend to regenerate
and then rise through it all, limpid and curious, as astronauts
step upon the lunar surface and as armies kill each other
without cease. Humans turn their thoughts toward Mars
and beyond, as the jellyfish sink down into the ancient shadow
where they have always gone, as if death were a form of sleep,
a dream from which they are revived, one lifetime to another,
cycling through the stages of life as the elastic architecture
of their bodies is made strange and new all at once. *Blooming.*

Starfields glimmer in the wavetops above. Sunlight scatters at dawn
and dusk. The ocean is a silver film of moonlight stilling itself.
And through it all, the jellyfish. The immortals. They have come
to watch galaxies loosen their spiraling stars as photons
shimmer on the interstellar breeze. They are steeped in time.
They have learned to reinvent themselves in defiance
of the body's undoing. They rise from their own deaths.
They rise from the bottom of the sea. Soft bells,
diaphanous and fine, the universe offers them wonder
and they gather in their multitudes to take it all in.

BEFORE/AFTER

1

A brachiated tree of lightning illuminated the oncoming storm
from its interior, then died out as quickly as it appeared. Rain,
bright and stinging, began to intensify on the Atlantic shoreline
as thunder rolled in over Africa. And the woman standing there?
She paused to consider the storm, her bare feet sinking
in wet sand as gusts of wind blew her hair in damp locs
and strands. This was 117,000 years ago, where her footprints
remain to this day.
            Of course, older relics survive.
I'm thinking of the tracks at Laetoli, in Tanzania—
the footprints of three human beings dated 3.66 *million* years.
Australopithecus afarensis. Our ancestors. Imagine them
on that journey through grasslands and mudflats, their prints
sealed in a tuff of rain and ash from a volcanic eruption.
Their tracks extend about eighty-eight feet, and nothing more.
They chart the narrative of a journey. They arrive
from the empty landscape, their footsteps appearing
out of that erasure before walking into their own oblivion,
mid-stride, each vanishing into the vault that gathers us all.

2

Imagine lovers turned to stone in the fiery ash of Herculaneum
as Mount Vesuvius eclipsed the sun with fire and smoke.
Consider the Incan Ice Age girl found on Mount Ampato. Or
the Egyptian dead from Luxor, wrapped in linen, sealed in resin.
Bog people mummified in the peat. The Haraldskjaer Woman.

Tollund, Grauballe, Nebelgard. Their stomachs filled with knotweed
and barley. The Egtved Girl. The Old Croghan Man missing his head.
And the Iceman, Ötzi, from five thousand years ago. If we unearth
the vast graveyard of our planet, from Homo sapiens to Neanderthals,
from Homo heidelbergensis to the use of fire with Homo erectus
about 1.5 million years ago, from the invention of cooking
with Homo habilis in the early Pleistocene to the stone tools
of Australopithecus to the chimpanzee split over six million years ago
and the use of bipedalism by the Orrorin and the Sahelanthropus
in the late Miocene, we find the Oreopithecus at eight million years
and the split with gorillas of the Ouranopithecus at nine million years
back, until, finally, we reach Nakalipithecus, which we know only
from three molars in a portion of a female jawbone, dated ten million years.

This wild family of ours. How patient it is, waiting for us in the earth.

   3
A couple of years before we met, I cupped an enormous ostrich egg
in my hands and studied a map of the world painted on its curving surface,
sealed in translucent lacquer. It was late afternoon. Hot. Damp. Kampala
rolling outward in every direction until it faded into the Ugandan countryside.
The music of minute flyers trilled the air. I held that globe and considered
where I'd been, where I was headed.

                          The streetlights of Kampala switched on
one by one. I thought of the Great Rift Valley, the migrations of human beings
throughout our existence as a species. I thought of the birds and wildlife
that did the same. And the more I pondered it—the more alone I felt.
The more untethered.

                    Whole years of my life spun across the globe
as I turned it in my hands. What I couldn't envision in that moment was *you*.
Or the year 2009. Do you remember? The night we stood in the Aegean,
the mountain village of Chora gone to dream on the island of Serifos.

I was thrilled and scared all at once, as the path fell into darkness
on each side, and I could only see you in front of me, soft-hued
and glowing, leading me forward.

Our feet pressed into the wet earth.
We leaned into the wind and climbed the slope of the mountain,
as blue-black and cold and silent as the sky—so that it felt as if
we had left the Earth as we knew it and learned to ascend
into the widening field of the universe.

I can hear the thrill of it in your voice even now,
so bright and brave, saying, *Can you feel it?*
Just stretch out your arms. We're standing in the stars.

SATELLITES

The universe, she's wounded
But she's still got infinity ahead of her
She's still got you and me

—GREGORY ALAN ISAKOV

When I was a boy, I slept on the lawn during summer nights like these.
Bats flew through the leaves of eucalyptus and stirred the air with cries

that washed over me in waves, the sound of their hunger baffled
by the damp cross-hatching of the grass. I stretched out

on that slender matting so I might catch the evanescent trail of a meteor
in descent. And while no organized religion has ever spoken to my soul,

those quiet nights stay with me. Synaptic, fleeting, strange. Each
fiery train. Each afterimage burning within. All the dead stars

and ancient rivers of light that have traversed the expanse of time.
The mystery of it housed within us. Deneb. Vega. Kochab. Altair.

Rigel. Antares. Sirius. Capella. They remind us of those we love.
Each of us, in the departure, alone. Such brief thoughts written across the sky.

HEROES

They are tiny heroes, small and unassuming, organisms
comprised of a solitary cell with a tail of minute filaments,
only 1.2 to 1.5 microns, far smaller than a red blood cell,
so diminutive and yet voracious in their hunger, capable
of ferreting out the carbon locked in the polymer of molecules
that form a resin known as PET, or polyethylene terephthalate,
which came into existence in the 1940s and has found its way
into most of human life—from clothing to tennis balls
to automotive parts to sleeping bags to the plastic bottles
racers jettison as the peloton emerges from feed zones
at the *Tour de France*, the same plastic we drank from
while crossing the salt flats in Utah in a summer long ago
or when we explored the streets of New York, Berlin,
Tokyo, and Tangier, replenishing ourselves with water,
with nearly one million bottles purchased every minute
of every day, the equivalent of half a trillion plastic bottles,
crowding landfills and polluting urban and rural landscapes
each year—with all of it eventually tumbling out to sea
to drift in the currents until they are gathered in a vortex
far out in the ocean, as in the Pacific Trash Vortex,
twice the size of Texas, and I am reminded that hunger
has a habit of adapting to circumstance, that hunger serves
as an antecedent to the molecule, driver of amino acids,
proteins, lipids, structures that rise from the periodic table
as if summoned by the earth and sea in a desperate plea
to bring a chemical balance back into this world,
and of course with such a monumental task at hand

it must be done by the smallest among us, the bacterium,
Ideonella sakaiensis, which secretes an enzyme to break down
the polymers in ways we desperately wanted chemotherapy
to mirror within the chemical environment of your own body,
where such fierce heroes were needed, and medicine's envoys
were sent to kill the cancer that entered the breastbone
and spread throughout much of your skeletal system, the bones
made porous, filled with so much ache and struggle, the cancer
sometimes blunted by variations of that *pharmakon* cocktail,
with a baseline transdermal patch of fentanyl applied to the wingbone
of your scapula every three days, year after year, and this mixed
with variations of Abraxane, bumetanide, cephalexin, cefuroxime,
cyclobenzaprine, diazepam, diphenoxylate, dronabinol, exemestane,
gabapentin, hydromorphone, iron, lorazepam, letrozole, metaxalone,
metoclopramide, morphine sulfate, nitrofurantoin, the serotonin receptor
antagonist ondansetron, sumatriptan, as well as oxycodone and OxyContin,
the aromatase inhibitor palbociclib, and potassium chloride, prednisone,
tamoxifen, tramadol—all of it swirling in your circulatory system,
your liver and kidneys processing it around the clock,
just as I imagine the bacteria when it was discovered
in a Sakai landfill, in the Osaka Prefecture, an organism so new
it lacked a name, this life-form which thrives in plastics,
invisible to the naked eye and yet fast at work saving the world
one plastic bottle at a time, breaking the semicrystalline structure
down to its constituent parts through the secretion of an enzyme
so that it might all be made new once more, or returned to the body
of the Earth in a form the Earth might recognize as the sweet-tasting
organic compound ethylene glycol, liquid and viscous,
as well as another organic compound, terephthalic acid,
first discovered in 1846 by a French chemist, Amédée Cailliot,
as an extract from turpentine, which is harvested from living trees,
from gum and pine wood forests of terebinth, Aleppo pine,

Sumatran pine, longleaf and loblolly, balsam and larch, trees
that could have never imagined what human curiosity and need
might do to them, the transformations they would undergo
to see the vision through, as well as this partial return, the bacteria
making it so, breaking down each bottle as if reversing history
at the molecular level, undoing the molecular chain to manifest the world,
as this bacterium, this new hero for our age, arrives with a hunger
that will not be sated, nor slowed in any way by the sheer scale
of the mountains we build—every minute of every day on Earth.

PLASMA

Do you remember that night spent in the cancer ward
grading essays past midnight—after the nurse inserted
a needle into the chemo port on your chest, that infusion
of plasma? A voice over the intercom announced each
incoming trauma in code, as a helicopter angled down,
hovering over a nearby rooftop, red lights flaring, the sky
deepening from cobalt to viridian as a cloud bank rolled in.
You sat upright in bed, with hospital pillows wedged
behind you, a privacy curtain sheltering us in a crescent
of undulating fabric hung from the ceiling. For a moment,
I thought of taking a photograph as you studied each page,
your eyes focusing on the construction of thought, the apt word,
the possibilities a sentence might evince, your pen scribbling
notes in conversation with your students as I sat beside you
holding back tears, gripping my hands into each armrest
as I witnessed your dedication to doing a thing right.
I had to catch my breath, then release it in a slow exhale.

You paused then, tucking the pen behind your ear.
Remember? I asked if it hurt to use the port,
and you said, *Oh, not this time, no, besides,*
I don't have to hope for a good phlebotomist
with this, and then your eyes followed the line
from your port to the plastic bag of plasma
hanging from the rack beside you, and you said,
Can you imagine—there are long-distance runners
in this plasma, tennis players, firefighters,

elementary school teachers and librarians,
social workers, I mean, just imagine
the strength assembled in this one plastic bag.
And as you said this your hands sculpted each
into the air right in front of you: distance runners
in motion, midstride, their legs like pendulums
sweeping a clock at the bottom of the hour;
dancers spinning their graceful limbs as you
helped guide each through the invisible, your palms
gentle, your head tilting as you welcomed them
into the hum and hush of the 8th floor, all of them
strangers, absolute strangers, each volunteering
the very blood coursing through their bodies.
And you said it reminded you of a fire brigade,
how these good souls had lined up to save you,
and the expression on your face as you said this,
the emotions catching up with you—
I'll never forget it, how vast
that store of gratitude, how beautiful
the tears that poured in that quiet little room.

FIFTY-SEVEN OCTAVES BELOW MIDDLE C

The note—which cannot be heard by the human ear—is a B-flat.
It's traveled across the expanse of space-time, over 1.3 billion light-years
and from somewhere in the general vicinity of the Milky Way.
There was a seven-millisecond lag from when this sound, carried
on a gravitational wave, first registered on the interferometer
at the massive, four-kilometer-long LIGO complex in Louisiana
before undulating through a sister complex in Washington state,
thousands of miles away—and so a reverse azimuth points us
toward a cataclysmic event: two black holes merging into one.

It was 5:51 a.m. September 14th, 2015. And in Florida,
the soft engines of our bodies curled into each other, entangled,
as that gravitational wave rolled through the frayed tips of our hair,
traveling through the amphitheater of bone and neocortex
as it washed through the seat of memory before rolling down
our spinal columns and into the curved housing of ribs embracing
our lungs, which paused for a moment, our breathing held fast
by the wave of this note sounding through the smallest structures
within, our hearts pumping claret and incarnadine at our very core.
We could only register this ripple at the atomic level, octaves
below our awareness, far lower than our own delta waves
that radiate within at 3.06 hertz as we sleep, as if our minds
hum in G, seven notes up from Middle C on the piano.

Did you know that black holes devour stars whole? And when they collide
they form still more massive structures. The largest known—J2157—
has an estimated mass equivalent to thirty-four billion suns—

and it absorbs one new star each day. I try to imagine it, but struggle
to comprehend the magnitude of it all. That blinding hunger.
The scale of such ecstasy, as the merging of these bodies
cries out with a sound that alters the fabric of space-time itself,
a transcendent echo rippling in every direction.

And yet. Who's to say that the same isn't true for us?
The sun rises. The sun sets. It arcs across the parietal dome
through an atmosphere of cerebrospinal fluid within us.
And we are showered in its light. Day by day by day.
We call it dream and we bask in its glow.
Each of us carrying as much of this life
as we can possibly hold. Rivers
pouring into the sea.

ANGIOPLASTY

This is how they travel through the body,
with a needle opening an arterial passageway
in your thigh, where I have laid my head to rest
on summer afternoons on a couch the color
of that August sunset we drove into, crossing
America, the road like a river that carried us
into the starfields of Wyoming. Remember that?
I'm in the waiting room now, drinking stale coffee
and scrolling through the news of the world,
but my eyes can't seem to focus, the words
blurring into bird tracks scribed in the mud
we waded into at Great Salt Lake, just
the two of us walking on a mirror of cloud
and sky, and surely this is what the doctors
find within you, the past in all its variations
of wonder, the days of a life we can count
one by one, with contrast dyes revealing it
as X-rays flood the images with light
and the camera, only 2 mm wide, explores
the interior of your body, the second hand
ticking forward until the moment, finally,
when I can brush your hair back, kissing
the sweet hollow of your temple, taste
the salt there, some memory from long ago, as you
return to the dull fluorescents and the sound

of gurneys wheeling patients and me, here,

welcoming you back from that underwater

landscape of anesthesia, giggling as you sing

> *I want to be*
> *under the sea*
> *in an octopus's garden*
> *with you*

INK

The radiation treatments started sometime after rounds
of MRIs, PET scans, X-rays. I don't have clear notes, or
a clear memory of this, as it was a time of fear, a kind of terror
rooted in the body and shared between us. We could feel it
in each other's hands as we held fast to one another
through a claustrophobic series of fluorescent rooms,
where doctors mouthed a language of contrast dyes,
barium, gadolinium, saline—and your quick jokes
about glowing in the dark and peeing
a nuclear stream of phosphorescent yellow
only landed once we were home again, our laughter
a softer medicine tamping the fear down in increments.

I don't remember us saying anything in the shower then.
The water poured over us, thrumming on our skin,
and you sluiced it through your hair. Your skin shone
with flaring lights, and the two of us stood there, glowing,
our bodies coated in a watery film. Each of us carried
the faint reflection of the other in our skin, as if our shadows
traveled into one another so that they might express the thoughts
we could not say aloud. Or things that *I* couldn't say aloud.
And you understood that. You knew I wasn't ready to hear
anything that sounded like a funeral. But maybe it didn't
need to be said. We could see it all in each other's eyes.

I studied the small black stars the radiologists marked
on your skin. Each haloed in a ring of ink, with lines
radiating outward from the circle in a gesture
to the four cardinal directions. The radiology team
sterilized your skin with rubbing alcohol before squeezing
a droplet of India ink there. A thin-gauge needle
pierced the outer layer at the center of each circle
to create a permanent tattoo on the rise of your right hip,
near each of your clavicles, and in the notch of your breastbone—
where your voice rises into the world. It was as if a constellation
were being mapped on your body. Mapped in India ink. This ink
believed to have been in use since as far back as the Neolithic era
in China, when the Stone Age gradually transitioned to agriculture.
It was made of lampblack and water then, with binding agents
added later. In the shower, this same ink bloomed in your skin.

I like to think I said something about how beautiful you were,
something about how it made sense that these tiny stars
had begun to appear, some recognition of the celestial,
the everlasting you within your flesh, but I wasn't
capable of speech. I simply paused over each star
with the pads of my thumbs lingering
as I eased soapy palms over your skin,
while the shower continued to shimmer
and slide over the curves of our bodies
before pooling at our feet.

CYGNUS THE SWAN

She glides through a milky river of stars with her wings
outstretched, magnificent, wingtip to wingtip spanning
seventy-seven light-years, a luminous body of feathers
brightened by deep space phenomena. She is made of these.
The Fireworks Galaxy. The Veil Nebula. The Crescent Nebula.
Pulsars, quasars, Messier objects—and more known planets
than in any other constellation, all spinning in their determined orbits.
The supergiant, Deneb, signals the Swan's wake, while Albireo
shines in her eyes—a star that is, in fact, binary, one candling yellow
while its companion is a lucent blue, the two burning into one.

A radio galaxy, the first ever recorded, broadcasts
from within the Swan with jets of energy streaming
from a pair of black holes. The impression is analogous
to the human body. That storage of memory. The way
trauma and delight funnel inward while radiating
outward all at once, pulsing in electromagnetic waves.
The bandwidth of these signals, once they reach Earth,
can be observable from 10 MHz to 400 GHz, then modulated—
so that frequency and amplitude of the waveform can be, yes, *heard*.

It's Tuesday morning in September, and you've just crossed over.
The Swan rows her way through that great river of light
as the yellow rain tree sways in the yard, each leaf
a small tongue of fire draughted by the breeze, as if
moved by the Swan's wings. It is a sight to behold.

Her wings stretched wide. Night into day and day into night. Even when I can't see her, she glides through the heavens right in front of me, her flight composed of fire and motion, feathers and wings.

ENEWETAK ATOLL

It's 1966. And in the Pacific, a breeze riffles
through the dry crowns of the coconut palms
as Marshall seals his mask. He's up to his chest
in the warm water of the lagoon, which fades
from a creamy turquoise to a marine blue
at its deepest point, 180 feet down. Cumulus
blooms to 7,000 feet before dissipating
into the atmosphere, the departure
of each body of clouds as enigmatic
and ephemeral as its formation.

It is a slow blue afternoon.
A ring of islets creates the nearly circular atoll,
Enewetak, which lies a few meters above sea level
at most, on a landmass that rose from the ocean floor
to become a seamount of basalt in the Cretaceous Period—
when pterosaurs soared on thermal updrafts
and their shadows cast over plesiosaurs
giving birth in the ocean below.

★

Marshall emailed me about it in late summer, 2012:

> Crystal clear water. Beautiful coral and fishes totally unafraid of humans.
> I once swam alongside a big sea turtle and petted its back—it swam faster
> than I could keep up with it. Swam alongside a stingray. Didn't attempt
> to pet it. Checked out some of the sunken tanks, landing craft, and other

detritus of the three-day battle for that tiny island. Never swam inside
one, out of respect for the dead, though I don't know that anything
would have remained of them after twenty years. Also didn't want to
come face to face with a shark in one of them. Schools of zebra fish and
parrot fish swam in and out, and down by the coral there were always
spiny sea urchins and the occasional toxic rockfish, both of which we'd
been warned against touching during our orientation.

At the orientation we were instructed not to eat the coconuts or any fish
we caught because they were radioactive due to an atom test back in the
fifties! It would be okay if we gave our fish catches to the Chamorros,
the fishermen who occasionally paddled to the east end of the island
at night. They'd make a fire and cook their—what else?—fish. I about
went into shock when I heard that—and to their credit so did the other
newcomers.

★

The fruit of the pandan tree, peeled of its husk, echoes
the burnt-orange sheen of the ocean at sundown. Soon enough,
steaks will sizzle on the grill, and Marshall and his buddy, Beauchamp,
drink from chilled bottles of San Miguel. The missions, the Russians,
the adrenaline, his own spy plane climbing into the atmosphere—
there will be time for all of this. There will be time to return stateside.
To start a family. For two daughters to be given names. A divorce.
A new marriage. A seven-year-old son. The decades passing by
until that son flies across country on an emergency flight
to see him in the last hours of his life, before Marshall is intubated,
a machine regulating oxygen into his lungs while his eyes
scan the room and those who love him gather in the ICU.
Each of us telling him how much we love him. Saying our goodbyes.

That was August, 2015. Almost a year before your own crossing.
And I couldn't talk with you about it once I came home.
I was a son who couldn't grieve. How could I? Imagine
how cruel that would've been. Instead, I had to push it all
down somewhere inside of me. Where Marshall is still.
Swimming. His mask cleared. A snorkel in his mouth.
There in the lagoon. In the blue mouth of a dead volcano.
In that watery pool of ink, where stingrays spread their silent wings
and fly beside him in the turquoise-colored water, as a bright ball of fire
burns dusk, burns dawn, burns each day down into the Pacific.

LAST, LAST THINGS

Here are the last waves of the ocean curling ashore.
One last glance toward the ancient source we carry within.
Horses galloping in the foam, shoulder to shoulder.
And the road home blurred green and vibrant with wind.
Our last best predictions about the future. That last
movie theater, coffee shop, restaurant. The last time
you sat behind the wheel, driving. And here are the leaves
on the last tree to turn gold. Your hands unfolding a letter,
the pen you hold as you reply. And here's the last wave
of broken hearts arriving cherry-red from a digital world.
And discursive conversations into the nature of the sublime.
The last painting, the last song, the last poem, the last piece of art.
And here are the last memories from Edinburgh, from the streets
and neighborhoods of your youth. And that figuration of strings,
that melancholy love, Rodrigo's Adagio. And the tears the music brings,
the bittersweet from long ago, that pathos, gone. And you kissing
a lover on a train platform, decades back, the goodbye kiss.
And you singing in the streets of Europe, a guitar case
clinking with silver. Your cheeks and fingers pinkened by the chill
as strangers turn to shadow and then vanish into history.

Winter, spring, summer, fall. The years disappearing, one by one.

And the exhaustion of the body in a tangle of sheets.
And the French vowels you tasted on another's lips. A lifetime
of lovers and friends you once knew, now strangers. The light
angling through the decades, diffusing, then gone. And all manner

of wild beautiful things that reside within. Even the bright flesh
of oranges bursting on your tongue. The sugars of this life,
so sweet when tasted last. A simple glass of water in your hand.

And the breeze off the lake. And the leaves trembling
in the rain tree out back. The chimes in the eaves, sounded
by wind. And that amber of daylight glowing in your hair.
The midnight rain and the meteors and the moon rising full.
The new moon and the pink moon and the hunter's moon falling.
The strawberry, the flower, the sturgeon, and the wolf.
The harvest moon we danced to and carried off to bed.
The last of the dusk that brought this last and final dark.
And the gardenias blossoming in the vase beside you.
An incense of lavender scenting the air with its perfume.
The candlelight wavering in the Buddha's palm.
The two us curled into the hours before dawn.
The last time you stood and walked into daylight.
The last time you stood and walked.
The last time you stood.

And the sound of my voice, low and broken, reading the words.
My hand holding your own when the time comes. And
the major organs failing, the body in its shutting down.
The lights within the cells beginning to dim and extinguish.
And the last of the cells in the brain, only minutes after
the last breath has gone by. The last of the heart,
the liver, the kidneys, gone after an hour. The skin
that housed you, the valves of the heart that beat so fast.
And the corneas, so stubborn, still trying to aid your sight,
well into the next day. And leukocytes, still fighting the invisible,
or trying to, three days gone. But before this, and just after
your very last breath—

my hands cupping your cheeks, smoothing your forehead,
the sobbing in my chest as my palms tried to hold you, that you might
stay, my love, impossible, all of it, the moment so fucking wrong,
though I might someday recall as beautiful, maybe, later,
but not now, here, in our bedroom, the world falling away,
your body so cold to the touch, your lips still soft as I kiss you
goodbye, and I feel you slipping further and further
into the ether, into the unknown, away, gone, I kiss you still
with all the sweetness and love that I am capable of,
the way I do with each return to this moment, another kiss
to carry with you in the crossing.

ANNA MARIA ISLAND

The beach is smooth and cool in the morning light, with a few silhouettes further along the shore that appear ethereal, wavering, as if composed of the ocean itself.

We hold hands and walk barefoot in the glassy window of the incoming tide. And while I've never told you this, I love the rising pitch of your voice when you say, *Oh, look,* and the plover-like strides of your legs as you chase after seashells tumbling in water and sand when the surf slides back out to sea. You collect lettered olive shells with their indecipherable messages etched into them. Banded tulips, Juno's volute, the sinistral shells of lightning whelks. *A malacologist's dream,* you say, *all of it.*

Mollusc shells form in three layers, with a mother-of-pearl interior turning into a prismatic middle layer that is coated, in turn, with a layer of protein called the periosteum. It's built inside out, with the nacre of the shell growing as the body within it grows—as cells from the epithelium, or mantle, secrete a matrix of crystalizing proteins and minerals. Calcite, aragonite, a polymer of conchiolin. Research has yet to fully understand it all, though the shells spiral logarithmically with an architecture and design that Descartes and Bernoulli described in the 17th century, expressing this in formulas that have evolved into this description of equiangular spirals—

$$\begin{cases} x\,(\theta) = r\,(\theta)\,\cos\theta \\ y\,(\theta) = r\,(\theta)\,\sin\theta \end{cases}$$

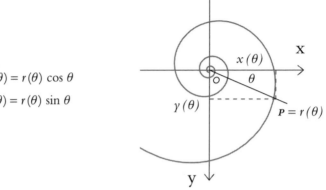

The math of it all is so precise, so visible. You can hold it wet and shining in the palm of your hand. It's a gesture to the infinite, I think, with similarities to the natural feature that fascinates me on our walks, too—the beauty and mathematics of the shoreline itself, both as a concept and as a physical presence. I'm imagining the salty foam at the lip of the tide. That boundary line of water and earth, land and sea. It's known as the coastline paradox—how the length of a coast depends on the unit of length used to describe it. The closer we observe the shore, the finer the detail we observe, the more it reveals its curves and fractals, the more it slips into the infinite.

And why wouldn't it be the same for the two of us? Why wouldn't the lessons of nature be written within us as well? The way we spiral into one another as we sleep, or when our fingers braid themselves into a weave of salt and water and heat. The way a moment, so fixed and simple in its composition, seems to fragment and dissolve into the wider landscape of time as one looks closer at it, here in the house of memory, where the figures further along the beach could be the two of us in the future, lovers returning to a shared experience, or simply walking along the shore, just as we are now, each a portion of the eternal, gathering the shells as they wash in, holding them wet and shining in the cups of our palms.

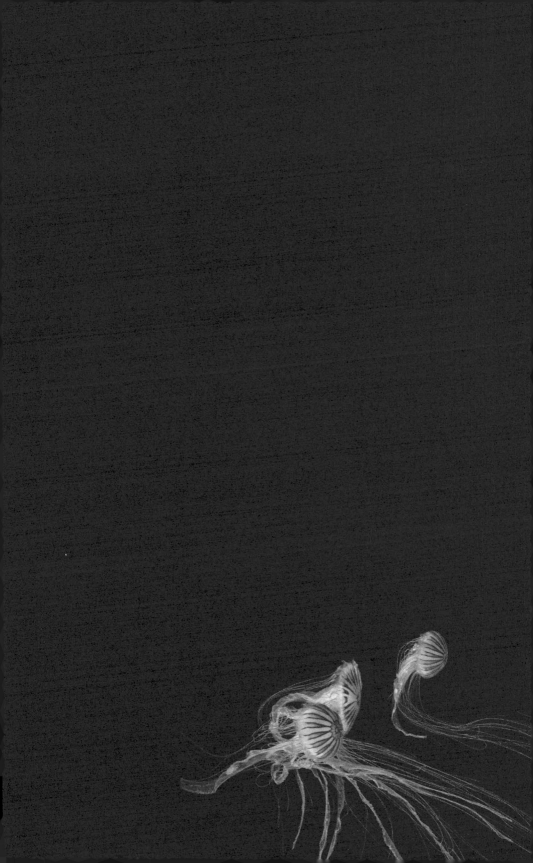

SEAGULLS IN CALIFORNIA

Did I ever tell you about the seagull? The one
flying in lazy circuits around me, counter-
clockwise, its wingbeats slow and steady, as I
sat on the shore, my vision glazed with dusk,
the ocean rolling in its waves of rust
as "Wish You Were Here" played from speakers
and my thoughts wandered through the past?

Did you know seagulls have a sense of humor?
At some point I realized the bird was trained on me,
its head cocked at an angle as I rested a forearm
on my knees, the fingers of my right hand brushing
the goatee on my chin, as if my thoughts gathered
to a conclusion there, and the bird mimed Rodin
then, stroking its beak with the talons of its right leg,
wingbeat by wingbeat circling until I finally caught
the joke, my head clearing of its smoky stupor,
and I laughed into the clear blue air.

I could say I was stoned, and dismiss the moment
by virtue of an altered state, but that would subtract
the sentience of the being in flight around me, and
it might return the bird to its status as object in motion,
as a feathered machine driven by hunger and instinct,
rather than an ocean flyer who paused on a beach
to witness a lost soul marooned on the shores of his life,
a young man staring into the sunset before he'd even

fully lived, despondent and certain he'd never discover
a lover who might also love him in return, and
that seagull, circling me on the beach that day—
it did the only thing it could, flying in circles
while locking its eyes on me until my body
broke open in laughter, until I was startled
back into this life once more, the bird
disappearing when I waded into the boom
of the surf, into the cool sheet of twilight
cast over the enduring waters of dream.

CEPHALOPODS

The genius of the octopus is so evident
as it escapes the fish tank designed to imprison it.

What better response than to imagine
a path over tile and grout, through a medium

of sky radiant with heat, flooded with sunlight,
here in the kingdom of shadow and acoustic

sibilance, where a susurration of voices funnels in
from a corridor beyond the laboratory, Science itself

chiseled into the sharp-angled nature of the room
this octopus must flee, the ocean wholly within

its imagination, though certain enough it would abandon
all safety at the very notion of it, simply for that blue joy,

fluid and serene, the pull of its currents urging the octopus
forward and through a landscape of human beings,

that it might view the stars from the cold depths
of the Pacific once more, that it might dwell

within itself, shifting its chromatophores and the texture
of its skin as the terrain requires, though now

there is only this flight, its siphon inscribing a cloudy trail
of ink in its wake, a message to its captors

that the word *beauty* exists within the octopus, too,
that here is the signature of personhood, if only

one were to make the effort to learn this
ancient alphabet, if only it might be read aloud.

THE SALTON SEA

Mosquitofish, red shiners, Mozambique tilapia, sailfin mollies.
Their mouths opened as if sustaining a long-forgotten note
once played on the wind, where the bleached skeletons
of dead fish drape over stones coated in a drying plaster
of saline-rich muck. Desiccated, frozen in place, tanned
to a leathery perfection. I scan the sun-scoured envelope
of air, and consider the tumbling fall of the bomb high above,
the pitch and wobble of it on descent toward its own reflection
in the waters below. The year 1945 falling alongside it.
I think of Colonel Tibbets flying practice runs in his B-29.
Each dummy round packed with concrete, stenciled with insignias.
Fat Men and Little Boys falling into a wide sheet of sunlight,
over and over. The speed at which they hit the surface.
The shorebirds startled into flight at impact.

★

I'm not sure how to fathom trauma when it's stored
in the Earth like this. And on such a vast scale.
I'm only beginning to learn what to do with pain and loss
when stored within the human frame. I'm reminded
of how the anger welled up in you. Remember?
You'd describe the Kirtland Air Force Base
on the edge of Albuquerque, your childhood there—
your hands mapping the landscape in front of you, gliding
down the Sandia Mountains and into the Rio Grande Valley
until they reached the lava escarpments and the aquifer

you drank from as a child. How the jet fuel spilled,
pluming underground. And your mother's cancer.
Your older brother's leukemia. The neighbor's cancer
two houses down. Stories shared neighbor to neighbor.
The lack of canvasing done in those neighborhoods.
The lack of responsibility. The stunning incompetence
needed, in the aggregate, to locate a base so close
to the water supply of a major population center.
Everything anecdotal and easily fading into silence.

And when people ask, and I say the word, *cancer*,
they nod and crimp their lips. Gravity pulls harder
on the air between us. But when I go on to say
it's possible you were poisoned by chemical pollutants,
that you were a casualty of the Cold War, one
of the many unrecorded deaths on the home front,
that's when even some close friends withdraw, nodding
slower, north to south. But maybe if I said there was
jet fuel in the groundwater? That it's still there?
Maybe if I said *ethylene dibromide*, a known carcinogen.
That most remediation attempts have been confined
to extraction of vapor from the soil. That the EPA
hasn't compelled remediation, or even thorough study
with core samples taken throughout the water basin
to grasp the extent of the plume within the aquifer.
Maybe if I said twenty-four million gallons spilled
into the water that Albuquerque rests on. Maybe
if I said it's among the largest underground toxic spills
in American history. Maybe if I said that.

CUVIER'S BEAKED WHALES

They hunt the deep for glass squid and giant grenadier fish,
ray-finned smelts and lanternfish, plunging almost ten thousand feet,
their breath held for over two hours at a time. As they sink, they wave
their flukes goodbye, something like the way you and I used to drift
off to sleep each night, our mouths opening in the blue dark.

What these whales cannot comprehend, or comprehend all too well—
the acoustic blasts of active sonar; submarines probing from 1-10 kHz.
In the open ocean, it's the sound of hunger. Cold. Metallic. Predatory.

Unlike humans, they listen through their throats, with soundwaves
traveling through channels of fatty tissue before entering their bony ears.
And when the Navy pulses its sonar, panic triggers within the whales,
a panic that drives them into the abyss or to the shore, the ascent
bringing on decompression—

> the bends, gas bubbles of nitrogen
> accumulating in their veins, internal vessels
> hemorrhaging in bronchopulmonary shock,
> their bodies disrupted at the cellular level,
> the spinal cord crackling
> with a searing, unrelenting pain

—and this is what spirits them to beach themselves on the shores
of an unlivable world, where they are bewildered, undone beyond
any reckoning, each animal suffocating as seagulls circle above,
the flukes and fins of these whales no longer of any use as the last
watery film evaporates from their highly-sensitive skin, each whale

changing hue as if turning to shadow, waves of sound muted

within them as this airy medium weighs them down,

their throats unable to amplify the strange figures

on approach, those with otherworldly voices

that register only at a faint decibel, with tones

so low and hushed and laden with dread

as they whisper and kneel before the whales,

touching each whale with such delicate palms,

with such tenderness, their fingertips tracing

the map of scars inscribed on the whales

as if reciting the whales' lives back to them

one last time before the lights of this world extinguish, one

after another, after another, after another, after another.

THE JURASSIC COAST

—Devon, England

Here is a portion of the silence we walk upon,
where the stony shore of the Atlantic curls
breakers of salt onto a shelf of the lithospheric dead.
At our feet, ammonites in their obsidian-colored whorls.
They seem to listen to the conversation of water and earth
with their strange ears made of stone, as if pondering
the after-effects of the Cretaceous-Paleogene extinction event
that occurred sixty-six million years ago. A rock hound
breaks them free with chisel and tap hammer, kneeling,
his shoulders hunched over the task. He holds the chisel
by the handle with his fingers crimped around the shoulder
of the blade to scrape along the ancient rim of an ammonite's shell.
It's a sound we've never heard before, though instantly recognizable—
that chawling of beveled steel against a seam of fossil, followed
by a ping of the hammerface until that bedrock cleaving is undone,
and a distant relative of the octopus is disinterred from its grave.

We pause to consider the near erasure of another ammonite fossil
through the application of water and time. What has become of it.
Mere gouges in stone. Its body now an image reminiscent of the sun
laid down, become art. And as we stand here facing the sea—
are we not also fading into the shore, into mountains and clouds?

★

It's now the year 2020, and the sixth mass extinction event
continues to alter life on Earth, unabated. This isn't hyperbole.
The International Union for Conservation of Nature
keeps a running list of species with less than one thousand
living in the wild, along with an annual Red List of species
on the brink of collapse. It's a kind of roll call of the dead
and dying. A casualty list for the Anthropocene. These losses
compound as extinction cascades revamp the ecological landscape.
Imagine the forests. Corals. Lakes and streams and tidal pools.
Wind-swept deserts. Grasslands. Tundra. Each acoustic space
diminishing. And then diminishing again.
The world that once was.

How do we mourn such loss?

How do we comprehend the vanishing of life
on a global scale?
The dying is so quiet.

We have to lean in and listen
just to notice it's even happening.

And how does one say goodbye to the addax and the Polynesian
storm-petrel, or the Malabar civet? Monday slides into Tuesday,
and then Tuesday slides decade by decade into a century of loss.
I close my eyes. This is where I say goodbye to the cherry-throated
tanagers and Saint Croix racers and green poison frogs.
The Rarotonga fruit-dove flies into the mist, followed
by little earth hutias and Chinese alligators and glow-throated
hummingbirds and black-winged trumpeters. The year 2030. 2050. 2100.
Say goodbye to giant pandas. Psychedelic rock geckos. Przewalski's horses.
Lava gulls and gharials and Bulmer's fruit bats. The *Cyrtodactylus chrysopylos*.

The northern river terrapin. Pangolins and red wolves and Sumatran rhinos.
Lange's metalmark butterfly. The echo parakeet sings only in memory
at this point, while Bonin flying foxes glide into a shadow
from which they never return. Galapagos pink land iguanas
dive into the ocean and the deep welcomes them in. Goldie's bird-of-paradise
and Vancouver Island marmots and black lion tamarins and Siamese crocodiles
vanish as if they never existed, listed only as statistics in research papers
buried deep within the archives of human thought. The Telefomin cuscus
never had a chance. And the giant kingbird, listed in the Encyclopedia of Life,
no longer sings from the pine barrens of Cuba. In the Solomon Islands,
a sombre leaf warbler trills back and forth from C to D to C
before singing its final note, liquid and sweet in the green boughs of morning.

These voices. They call out across the landscape of time.

★

I'm reminded of the last passenger pigeon, Martha,
who died at the Cincinnati Zoo over a century ago, in 1914.
She was frozen in a block of ice and shipped to the Smithsonian,
where a taxidermist prepared her body for public display.
Her wings folded in close. The downy curve of her head
angled to the right while she clasped a branch in her talons.
Now a passerine within the Objects of Wonder exhibit. She's listening
for the call of a lover, a voice that no longer sings over the grasslands
and woodlands of North America, while her eyes, ever open, focus
on some distant point, where she remembers how the sky
appeared cloudy due to the inexhaustible numbers of pigeons,
an entire nation of flyers once numbering between three to five
billion, once reported to have stretched a mile wide in its migration,
the flight of these birds passing overhead for hours on end.

THE END OF THE WORLD

I wanted the ruin. I'd be lying if I said otherwise.
I wanted that hurricane to destroy what was left of my life.

But when Hurricane Irma, a name that means *the world*,
made landfall on the Gulf Coast of Florida, with Collier County
absorbing the brunt of it with the storm shifting direction
sometime after the dead of night, its wind speed diminishing
as it rolled over central Florida before leaving our home
nearly untouched—I was relieved.

But I was also, deep down, *fuming*.

I'd wanted that storm. I'd wanted those howling winds
to blow off the roof and carry me tumbling through the air
like some dying swimmer flailing over the neighborhoods
of Orlando. Or, if that hurricane simply crushed me to death
and then splintered the home around me into an unspeakable
puzzle of what was once our favorite place on Earth—so be it.

Of course, it is what hurricanes do. They wheel and churn
and open their eyes to stare, as if through a giant magnifying glass,
at any living creature trapped in their sight. Irma was a Cape Verde,
which began when a low-pressure trough moved beyond the archipelago
four hundred miles off the Senegalese coast. Reconnaissance aircraft
measured the eye wall at twenty-nine miles in diameter. The wind shear
favorable, ocean surface temperatures warm, with a storm system
north of Irma steering the hurricane on a west, southwest path.

It's a kind of corridor of storms that I've learned to recognize
over the years, as clouds cross the Sahara to ride the wind out
over the Atlantic, and then the swirling begins, that gathering
of moisture, the lifting of the ocean into a roiling hurricane
with the eye forming and reforming as the storm becomes
disorganized, as if troubled in thought, before opening its eye.
With Irma, radar revealed an elliptical eye and double eye walls
as the hurricane cycled past Puerto Rico and, as a CAT 5, blew
over Cuba with sustained winds of 165 miles per hour. Hurricane hunters
flew at ten thousand feet over the storm, deploying dropsondes to collect data
on wind speed, direction, dew point, latitude, longitude, atmospheric pressure.
Each dropsonde—tethered to a small parachute—fell 2,500 feet per minute
while pulsing out data every two seconds. Irma churned in a path
forecast to pummel our home. Oaks and golden rain trees would snap,
the roof would be ripped away, the ocean come pouring from the sky,
and the howling and the thunder and the lightning would destroy
the artifacts of our lives. Every photograph. Every piece of paper
with your handwriting. Every item of your clothing slipping free
and whirling into the closing eye of the storm, one after another,
as if so many versions of you were dancing into the air, as Irma,
so determined in the task, nearly carried us away.

CLOUDS

Time has begun to gather in ways I cannot fully comprehend, with weeks folding
into months, seasons, entire years layered in striations, one after another, and in
each of the past 1,318 days since that Tuesday morning in September when the
constellation of the Swan crossed the horizon at dawn through a river of stars, I've
been looking for you in our house, in the poems you left, the birds at the window,
in the surprise of messages left in various ways, just as you'd promised, and also,
though we hadn't talked about it—high up in the atmosphere, where the heat of
the Earth and the intentions of all manner of plants and animals, the kingdoms of
leaf and fin and feather and muscle and soil join together in a column that rises
into the ether to engage in a conversation with the dead, and the dreams of the
dead, that landscape you have crossed into, there in the clouds, in that transitory
state of being, that meditation of hydrogen and oxygen as each molecule fastens
itself to the finest particulates of matter lifted by wind and carried aloft over the
curvature of the globe, which some might simplify as sleet or snow or rain, as if
the crystallization of ice could be a mere scientific fact and not a point of wonder,
as if the possibility of rain within that ice could not also be connected to a source
of pain, or sorrow, or joy, as if the tears that poured out of us that last month, and
the morning we cried in each other's arms when that last phone call brought
the oncologist's final words into our very bedroom, as if those words and those
moments are not part of what shifts and moves through the billowing structures of
clouds, cumulus clouds, with their quiet meditations that cross the sky, no matter
how accustomed we might become to them, how typical and inconsequential they
may seem, as if mere acts of chemistry performed in a blue medium on a warm
afternoon, the weight of each cloud somewhere just over one million pounds, and
yet, even with such impossible weight, with so much to carry, they float and drift
on the invisible, an insomniac's delight, pouring rain from so high it is difficult to
trace the source, where the lightning flashes and the thunder rolls outward no matter

my sleeping form below, or maybe because of it, and the smallest raindrops there, some as slight as $1/16^{th}$ of an inch fall into others as the water wells in the descent, which is in the nature of sorrow and joy, the rain gathering to the point where the air pressure below begins to press up against each droplet and—if one were to look close enough—they might appear like translucent miniature parachutes, these parachutes of rain falling in uncountable numbers before breaking up into smaller droplets once more on descent, the rain falling twenty miles per hour, about ten meters per second, which is dramatically slower than a human being falling through the sky, about five times slower, which owes less to the physical forces of gravity and the act of drag on bodies moving through space than it does to the dreams that form the rain to begin with, the visions of the dead crossing over the state of Florida, our own dreams in conversation there as I sleep in our bed and the forces of gravity are undone by the landscape of the imagination and the wild terrain of the soul, which I have witnessed from time to time, mostly on warm, sunny days, when I catch glimpses of you high over the Earth, a breeze washing sunlight over the features of your face, your hair blown back, the shadows deepening under your eyes and then softening in recognition of my concern and worry, your skin the color of stone, then rain, then peaches and sugar pouring through your expressions as your thoughts shift, the way clouds do, with so many of the dead clamoring for a moment of this visual language, its sculptural vernacular made of light and vapor and love, love the very source of it, as well as the water composing each face and figure, the water a gift, a loan we all share, the human body an echo of this work of clouds, as the water that mourns and lives within me will likewise one day speak from high up in the air as these clouds do now, just as the dust that rises from the Earth is composed not only of granite and shale and quartz, whole mountains and entire epochs of the Earth crushed into dust that might float and rise into the wind, into clouds, that dust is also made of hair and skin and nail and tooth, the ash and flake of bone rising from the chimneys of loss, with all of it seeding the rain, the generations that fall from miles above, the dead, the clouds, *you*, my love, and all I need to do is wake, to rise from our bed and walk out into the storm rolling in from the Gulf, the wild trees brushing the night around me as your face turns silver with lightning, then blue and charged and glowing, the two of us seeing each other once more, and from within you the water pouring its language, the way it always has, pouring through the empty sky as I lift my face to you, to the rain coming down cool and sweet as your lips kissing me with it, the infinite pouring its silver parachutes over the world and every dreaming thing in it, until I am drenched in moonlight and rain.

THE AUDITORIUM CAVE

—Bhimbetka, India

Archeologists often describe vast waves of time
as occupation layers, or horizons. In this particular cave,
we have to peel away layers of historical sediment
until we arrive at the Upper Acheulean Horizon, or
even deeper into the Lower Chopping Tool Horizon.
Once we've traveled far enough, the excavation reveals
cupules—rounded indentations in the interior of the cave.
They are rock markings pounded into crystallized quartzite.
Imagine what it would take to create any one of them.
The sheer number of blows. A hammerstone held in the palm
and pounded against the wall of the cave, over and over,
with precision. And while some might call it art,
or a message to the gods of thunder to pour any rain
they might hold within the ever-changing bodies they cloud
across the sky, I think it might have been the pounding
of one's sorrow into the wall of the mountain they lived in.
A hammerstone swung against all that is resolute.
Each report sounding itself deep into the mountain.
Percussion petroglyphs. Forged within the cold
and indifferent. The stone altered by it.
Made to embrace its own silence.

As it often happens. We recognize absence by what holds it.

And how could this not be considered art? Painful
though it may have been to create. Pounded
into the mountain 290,000 to 700,000 years ago.
The sound of it ringing throughout the cave, even still.

*

I'm reminded of our home in College Park.
Built in 1949, I doubt it will see the year 2100.
At some point, it'll be torn down in a matter of hours,
its footprint cast over in concrete for another
housing generations to come. None of them
will have the slightest clue that we lived here.
That we even existed. In their busy lives,
they likely won't pause to consider what once was.
The two of us dancing in the kitchen. Spinning vinyl
until dawn. Crying in each other's arms. Laughing.
That floating in the dark we did in bed, drifting
hour by hour through wavelengths of being.

And these new people, those who come after—
I imagine them in bed at 2 a.m., in a room
a few stories above our own. One of them listens,
breathless for a time, then gently wakes the other,
as you used to do sometimes, leaning in
close, whispering—*Do you hear that?*

ASHES, ASHES

California is on fire. And the beauty of it is undeniable.

The ash content in the atmosphere creates gorgeous sunsets over the still waters of Lake Tahoe—where I stand on its northern shore considering the aperture settings on my camera, the precise amount of light to harvest through a polarized filter.

At night, I dream of ash falling from the sky.

The parts per million. Forests and plant-life reduced to cellulose, resins, starches, tannins. Hydrocarbons. Carbon dioxide. Water vapor. An entire forest lifted into the blue ether and held aloft just long enough for the sunlight to consider it once more, as if nostalgic for what once was, as if listening for the birds that sang in those high canopies, or a San Joaquin kit fox lifting its head to call on a silent god in the starfields above. Sagittarius watches on, as does the asteroid, 2212 Hephaistos, seated in a smithy of light.

The longest burning fire on Earth is located some two hundred miles north of Sydney, Australia, at *Burning Mountain*. It's an underground coal seam fire estimated to be six thousand years old. According to legend, a widow implored one of the gods to kill her because her sadness was too great to bear. The god refused, and instead turned her to stone. It's said that tears of fire fell from her—and that the fire pooled beneath her inside the Earth. Her figure reclines along the ridge of the mountain to this day. It is her great and enduring loss that burns century by century.

Of course, our home, Earth, rests on a mantle of molten metal. Basaltic. Andesitic. Rhyolitic. *Magma*. If we live long enough, and if we care enough, each of us will lie down in our own stony silence, with a pool of fire below.

My father's body was transported to the crematorium during the first week of September 2015. We were told it would be a few days until the morticians could cremate him because there was a backlog of clients queued up ahead. I tried to picture the space, that small warehouse of the dead awaiting transfiguration, and an underground grotto came to mind—like the catacombs of Rome or the dusty underworld of Paris. Only this was Fresno, and so I imagined a modest-sized gallery, a few torches lighting the tableau, and the dead, of course, lying side by side, luminescent in their silence. My father, white-haired and stern-faced, surely irked by the ineptitude of work taking place around him, remaining attentive to the sound of the oven door rising open like a guillotine and sliding shut. Or maybe it resembled the inside of a bullet. Something pointed toward a god and given ignition. I imagined the lifting of bodies. The last words, sometimes. One last check for rings or false teeth or anything forged in metal before the bed glides into that final housing. Gloved hands backing away. Then the chamber's intake of oxygen, the roar of fire muffled by sheets of metal, and the gaseous residue that lingers in the air afterward. A fire of such intensity even vapor is broken down at the molecular level and electrons pushed outward to distant shells the way planets drift further and further away from a sun that's lost its gravitational pull.

My father's body, singular and human, given to the air.

Cremation normally happens during business hours. That fact alone goes against my imagination, which pictures the practice as a duty for the graveyard shift. Instead, the ovens are brushed out and heated up as coffee percolates in the break room. The dead, wrapped in blue plastic bags, are boxed in cardboard that is taped shut and then housed on storage racks. Normally, the morticians will slide one of the boxes from the rack and onto a stainless-steel table with metal casters before wheeling it onto a scale for measurement and then on into the cremation room itself.

They wear latex gloves throughout this part of the procedure, as well as surgical masks and headgear, but once inside the cremation room they don Kevlar with aluminum backing, gloves that can withstand 1000 °F. Once the body is fully inserted into the chamber, the operator depresses a button and the outer door slides down to seal the heat within. There is a small view port, a kind of spyglass into the body's undoing, and those who haven't witnessed a cremation are most often captivated by what they see. It's the beauty of the fire that draws the eye. The signature of the body stripped of form through a travail of fire. The reduction. The incineration. The disappearance. Not the metal rakes or the carbon steel bristles afterward. Not the processing station with its rotary saw blades. It's the fire that pulls us in.

Within the confines of welded steel, jets of flame work to turn tissue and fluid and bone into ash. The temperature needs to reach between 1400—1800 °F and it often takes a little over two hours to complete this stage of the work. The bones glow in the fire. They ember and brighten. And as much as I try not to, I can't help but imagine my father's skull at 1600 °F with twin rivers of flame rising through the orbits of his eyes.

The world is trying to teach me about dying.

Something about the covalent bond, the narrative of the body inhabited by the soul.

About the canvas of dead stars burning in the heavens above.

2

I slept with your ashes the night you came home.

I knew it was morbid and pitiful, but I curled around the box and cried and talked with you and, at some point, exhausted, fell asleep.

Actually, that's wrong. I didn't think it was morbid or pitiful. I curled around you and held you as best I could. It made no sense at all and yet it made complete sense. The carved wooden Buddha in the corner of the room glowed in candlelight, and those small flames shifted gently from left to right as if a hand calmly passed over them, and the Buddha's face warmed in the slow-moving waves of heat radiating from the candlelight below.

A sharp and unmistakable jab to my rib cage startled me awake. It was so sudden I found myself sitting upright, searching across the room. I had distinctly heard a voice, *your* voice, just before being jabbed, saying, "Get *up.*" I even sensed your frustration, as if you'd been trying to wake me for some time.

I've awakened to the fact that my life is on fire.

My house is on fire. The grass in the yard is made of green tongues of flame, just as the banana leaves unfurl in flame and the angel trumpet bells open in petals of fire. It's not something I would've ever thought possible, not even remotely, but you get used to the heat. The window blinds ripple and furl with rays of sunlight burning through. The faucet in the sink filters a gel of fire to fill the glass I drink from as I watch the cardinals through the kitchen window. The roofing pops and cracks in fire day after day, while the yellow rain tree leans over, almost comforting, its branches flushed with songbirds.

The brightness is a different story. The glare off the windows keeps me up at night. The neighbors pause on their front doorsteps to note the natural ebb and flow of this fire, like scientists charting a coal seam blaze. The firelight reflects off other people's faces. At the coffee shop, the barista accepts my change before observing the residue of ash it leaves on her palms, then smiles professionally while inwardly questioning how I don't just kneel down and turn to cinders and dust right there on the spot.

I am the man on fire who lives in a house of fire. I begin to perceive a few others like me, others who pass by on the sidewalk or drive by in their cars, and there is a moment of recognition, a trail of smoke in their wake. We burn. We smolder. But there is nothing for me to learn from them, and what could I possibly say that might prove of any worth to them?

My life is on fire. Green tongues of flame burn to ash all around me.

ANNA MARIA ISLAND

Did you know that the common housefly, like the one circling the room now in a wide, counter-clockwise circuit, hums in the key of F? It's true. They come in different sizes, of course, but their bodies scale so that the vibrations of their wings correlate to the pitch intervals in F major: *F, G, A, Bb, C, D, E*. The octave above. Their wings are made for this.

I didn't know that back in 2015. There was so much I didn't know, like you only had one year left to live. We stood beside each other in the kitchen and prepared a dinner of rice and melted cheese, your favorite, as it reminded you of childhood, a rare pleasure from back then, and it helped ease the nausea from the row of pills you'd laid out on the table.

We told each other that we were living with cancer. That this was possible. The monsoon rains poured down as thunder rolled over the peninsula from the Gulf Coast to the Atlantic Seaboard. We'd rented a cottage on our favorite beach, with sliding-glass doors opening onto a sandy path that wound through iceplant dunes and soon gave way to tufts of sea oats and, fifty meters out, the salt of the tide curling into the boom of the surf.

I drank from a bottle of coconut rum. The rum added a sugary sizzle to our lips when we kissed. I can feel the tips of my fingers at the small of your back even now. Your hair brushing the side of my cheek. The fragrance of your hair after floating in the warm waters of the Gulf, hour after hour. The salt of the ocean on your skin.

There were days like this. Whole afternoons lived in suspension. Floating. Ruin stalled-out and gliding on its own silence, somewhere off in the distance.

The housefly circles past and I've returned to another unlivable year, 2020, with this fly humming in B-flat as I stare out the kitchen window. Its flight path is reminiscent of the Earth's orbit around the sun, and the note reverberating in its wings has a bittersweet timbre to it. Vivaldi, I think. *The Four Seasons.* It was composed with the sound of flies written into a figuration of notes, in F major, maybe the only time flies have appeared in classical music. And this housefly, so singular in its hypnotic focus, banks around me as though trying to spin me backwards in time while signaling the coming of fall.

But that earlier fly, the one on the coast in our little love nest on the ocean—*that* fly was drunk on the moment. Its wings hummed along to "The Girl from Ipanema" as it swooned in the damp ocean air, dizzy with circling two lovers who circled each other, dancing. With a lifespan of only fourteen days, it swam around us as we spun in the kitchen and laughed, the thunder rolling over and past and on toward some day we hadn't landed in yet. Each grain of rice expanded with water as the heating element began to glow on the stove. Tree frogs sang to the storm outside. Inside, the two of us were multiplied in that fly's vision, as the common housefly has between three thousand to six thousand simple eyes that comprise each of their two complex eyes. So many versions of us walked barefoot through the doors and into the rain. Kissing. Dancing. Laughing. And that fly's tiny yet intricate brain gathered in each and every one of us. However incomplete. However fragmented. This a definition of love on Earth.

The fly would have *these* memories to think back on, after we packed up and drove home. That's when the fly, resting on the windowsill, stared at the blue-green swells of the ocean rolling in, the sound of it muffled by panes of glass. The muscles in its legs slumped forward, then gave out. And maybe that's when the fly remembered you saying that—as a young girl—you'd seen horses in the curling salt of the wave when it crashed, galloping ashore. Uncountable horses. And when the fly looks for them, it's true, there they are—with manes of salt pulled back by the wind, the horses shoulder to shoulder, galloping in.

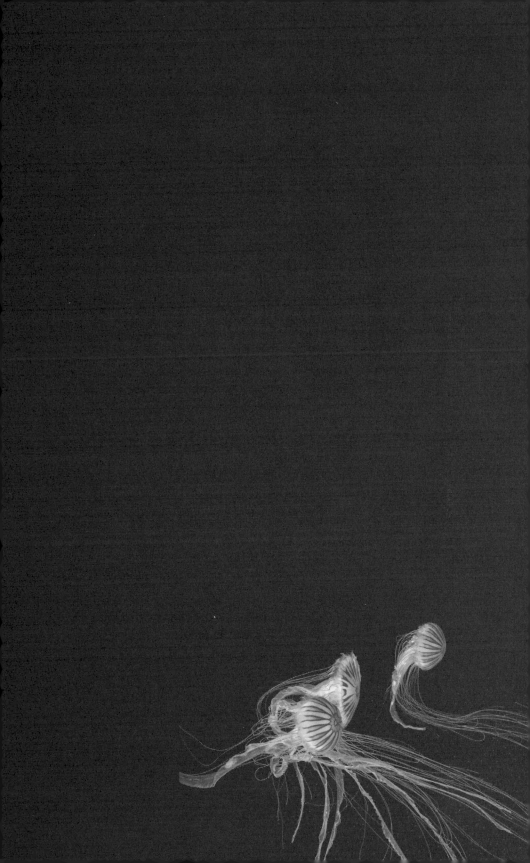

MOUNT FARAWAY

Noctilucent clouds shimmer in the twilight of the mesosphere
until they are subsumed into the blue-black field of night.

Each hour folds into the next while the crystalline wakes of meteors
articulate an unfinished language in the sky, though Earth's atmosphere,

spinning, blurs each word beyond recognition. And the wind,
ever relentless, blows the month of February across the snow flats

and up into the rocky crests of the Theron Mountains. In the scree,
in a pocket hollow that blunts the windchill, a pair of snow petrels.

They angle their heads and shiver, giving each other knowing looks,
as lovers often do when I pass by. And why wouldn't they? Here I am—

a lone astronaut trudging up a mountain of snow and ice in a space suit,
calling to the wind and stars, though my voice circles and dies out

within the globe of my helmet. The petrels are reflected in the visor
when I look over at them, and it's something that disturbs them,

though they might not register this on a conscious level. The petrels
consider me as I lean into the wind, the grave force of its currents

like an invisible river, as the Earth speaks to me through the cold voice
of winter. A voice that chills to the bone. And my pulse weakens

as my heart pounds its drum of muscle and valve and blood. Neurons
flare throughout the mind, though my fingertips and toes numb in the chill.

And my vision assumes an aspect of film, so subtle I wonder
if erasure is in the landscape or in me. The petrels blink, then

look away when I turn to see them. It's how strangers avert their eyes
at the sight of me, as I am a reminder of what their love portends, no matter

how fast they may have flown, how parallel the flight, how exhilarating
the bright rushing beauty of two bodies in tandem diving cliffside into the blue.

I cannot deny the resentment. The warehouse of anger I hold.
And while others might see only the sadness, the way I trudge on,

the way everything I do seems watermarked with the word *after*—
I also find it thrilling. That love exists. Even now. The globe itself

thrumming with it on a planetary scale. Even in the most unlikely
and austere of places, as it is among petrels in the desolation of winter.

It may be a symptom of hypothermia, this slow dying I call my life,
but I find sweetness in the sight of lovers when the day blurs

and disappears around them. That electricity. Those blue sparks
firing in the cold air. The way they kiss and the universe pauses

to register the moment on the grand scale of time. I'm transported by it.
I'm reminded of you. Of the two of us.

And this is what I didn't expect. That the world would help me to survive
after. That it would do so by revealing *you* within its myriad forms.

By feather and leaf and tangle of fur. Through water and air and fire and stone. That I might find a way to continue falling in love with you, and that

I might do so by remembering how to fall in love with the world itself.

CRYOGENIC

At 320 °F—below zero—the severed head of Ted Williams
    remains frozen within a welded tank of liquid nitrogen.
This is in Scottsdale, Arizona, where his eyelids are closed
    in the dark, as if in dream, as if recalling the sunlit days of a life,
his mouth opened to recite the things he's learned from the journey
    of days and months and years, his last breath exhaling *forever*
until Mary Shelley whispers in his ear—*Dr. Frankenstein's returned,*
    he's here to stitch you whole once more, to apply the lightning
that might reanimate you, so you can wade into the wide river
    of memory to cast a line over the blue waters of your life.
Is it all so strange? How desperate we are to remain, to feel,
    to be carried by the current on our journey toward the sea
where the broken sun dazzles in brilliant multitudes, that we might live
    beyond the limits of the body, to be awakened in a century
our own age could only imagine. And am I any different?

There is an orange, round as a stitched ball and sealed in a Ziplock bag,
    and I've saved it for years now in the freezer in the kitchen
at the back of our house. It's the last orange of your life. The one
    you never had a chance to eat. The globe of its fruit
awaiting you still, as yet unpeeled, its soft interior, its bright sugars.

WAITING FOR THE SUN

After days of rain, wind howling swells of the Beaufort Sea
onto the rocky shoreline with a spray of salt and spume,
the rain turns to sleet and then sleet turns to snow
on the 141st meridian, where the border with Canada
points to the Earth's axis. And frozen under an icy crust—
Canadian wood frogs practice the art of dying.

In winter, their bodies freeze through and through,
their internal fluids crystallizing, and that's when
they cross over, as a herpetologist might affirm,
into the kingdom of the dead. Brain functions
effectively slow to zero. Their hearts stop.
Their lungs grow cold. Stilled in frost. Icebound.

When I place my head to the pillow and stare
into the gloaming of my life, I wonder
if this frozen death isn't deep within me, too.
Do you think of this? Do you hear my voice
when I whisper in the dream-dark of our room?
I think back to the morning of your death
in 2016, the world closing around us.

The windows are glazed in blue sheets of light.
The doors locked in their metal housings.
My heart slows, my breath turns shallow.
What is it that wakes me from all of this?

What will you tell me, hours from now, as I work
to perfect the art within me? What is it you whisper?
What kiss do you bring to my lips to spark the muscle
on its frame of bone, charging the blood with a voltage
connected to memory, where bright fires burn
in the wide amphitheater of the brain, and we
are together again, you laughing, the calendar
returned to a lazy Sunday afternoon, the paint
from last night staining your fingertips, the painting
of flowers over our bed overflowing with petals, fragrant
with color, and, of course, this must be what melts the ice
from deep within the body. This must be what awakens
the frogs in spite of the wind arriving from the Arctic.

The frogs must know what can only be learned
in a silence so deep it stills the heart, quiets the blood.
When the spring comes, or maybe in early summer,
they will open their eyes. Encased in ice, they'll stretch
and slip into the faint light of day—to witness
the migration of caribou across the warming earth,
to see the smoky exhalations from those shaggy creatures,
and decipher meaning from the clicking sounds of caribou
as they hoof through a slush of mud and crushed ice
before softening into shadow and disappearing
into the low-hanging fog of morning.

Mosquitos lift from their fragile stations then. Their wings
lacy and patterned by veins. A faint shimmer of light
as they wheel and turn on the breeze. And the frogs,
having returned to this world once more—
crane their heads and open mouths wide.

They gather the cool air deep inside and,
with all that they have learned from the silent place
they have traveled to in dying, they sing.

ONE LAST MOMENT IN THE VAST CITY OF ANTS

With subterranean housing for millions, it's an abandoned city now,
left vacant. Imagine the labor it took to tunnel through, to carve out
each massive vault and to press forward, toiling without cease,
undaunted by the unyielding earth, resolute in the task, ants
tunneling passageways from one season to the next, each
with a lifespan of sixty days, at best, and still they pressed on,
generation by generation digging further into the sediment,
their claws and mandibles dismantling the hours set before them,
each destined to perish without seeing the vision to its end,
each glimpsing, perhaps, a sweeping monument of architecture
that later rendered scientists speechless by the scale of it.
Sunrise to sunset. Civilization by civilization.

When the city was alive with ants, the rains brought deluge,
storm-driven panic. Those on the surface were pummeled
by raindrops as large as the ants themselves, the water falling
through the empty sky from 2500' above. Weak and strong alike
were carried away by floods, never to be seen by the colony again.
Those in the tunnels faced a torrent of water funneling down
with no end in sight, the roar of water and gravity their doom.

When scientists discovered this combed structure at their feet,
they poured several tons of concrete into vents and entryways—
flooding the passages and chambers below. Anything dead or alive
instantly entombed in liquid stone. Crews then removed the soil
in an area covering roughly five hundred square meters, eight meters

deep. They struggled to comprehend the planning, the logistics, the social organization necessary to see it done.

In Brazil, where the excavated city lies open to the air, I imagine one solitary ant pausing near the trees where the horizon-line meets the sky. A small river of ants pass by, steadfast in their labor and intention. And that lone ant, as curious a creature as I am, looks back along the path as it chews a fibrous green leaf, angling its anvil-shaped head now and then to consider the wind swaying blades of grass in the valley below. Like some whisper of the past. Some echo from long ago. Some old story about a city lost in the earth, where the ancestors once rose in their multitudes to take flight, a calamity in their wake which no one can remember pushing them on into the green world still.

HYPERION

The fires of 2020 have burned their epitaphs into history.
In the redwood forests of California, on the far side of winter,
snow falls in slow drifts through the ancient crowns that disappear
in mist. It is a grove of giants, with an understory of burnt madrone
and tanoak, laurel and red alder, sword fern returning with blade-shaped
chevrons of green. Roosevelt elk graze on the fresh leaves of sorrel
unfurling from stems rising through char. Pine martens hunt
among the deadfall of the younger trees and the clustered trunks
that magnified the fire's heat, much of it reduced to a crush of ash.

Overlooking it all, at 379.1 feet, Hyperion, the tallest tree on Earth.
It is six to eight hundred years old, from the genus *Sequoia sempervirens*.
I close my eyes. Breathe in the sweet perfume. A wandering salamander
rests on a matting of moss, sliding its tongue under a globe of dew
to guide it into its mouth—as if drinking a liquid portrait of the forest.

Remember the carved wheel of a redwood we once saw?
Twelve to fifteen feet in diameter, that horizontal slice was displayed
so that we could walk up and touch its raw interior, its history.
The droughts. The good times. Years of green and gold scribed
in concentric circles, with centuries of life detailed in the heartwood.
It was something like a vinyl record turned on its edge, and you said—
If we could play it somehow, imagine what we'd hear. Your fingertips

traced the grooves. And as I think of this, I hear the birdsong in the mist.
Hermit warblers. Dark-eyed juncos. Otherworldly voices feathering down.

How wistful the trees must be, and heartsore, considering us.
We are given such a brief time to love. A few years, only.
Moments. Some of it archived within the trees themselves.
The way our voices whispered as the falling snow erased
the flame-shaped leaves, dampening the cross-hatching
of mulch at our feet. The things we shared. Secrets.
The way we lifted our faces and closed our eyes
to listen. The way our fingers braided together
as we walked into the silence of the grove.

KISSING IN THE RAIN OF NEW YORK

And infinities stretch out from infinities within
And I'm a part of everything, I'm a part of everything
—MARTIN CRAFT

We were so new to each other. The hours could still be counted
on our fingers. And yet. The misty rain set like dew in your hair.

Midtown Manhattan thrummed electric from the East River
to the Hudson while a woman draped in stone waited in the harbor

with a burning lamp held out toward the open ocean.
And across the street—the hotel where we'd soon make love.

It's a memory I visit often. Quiet as a ghost, the way we are
with the past, fading in and fading out. Sometimes I stand

on the opposite side of the road. Others I'm close enough
to watch your hands curling around my back, my palm

cupping your cheek, my fingers threading into the silky
roots of your hair as we tilt our faces into each other's light.

How alive we were. How present. The city's soft fires
blurred around us in fluorescent tubes and bulbs shaped

like raindrops made of glass. Cars drove past with a sound
of the ocean in the sluicing of water through their treads.

The science is not in on this, but I can't help thinking
quantum entanglement exists. That our bodies began

a conversation that night which hums within me to this day.
And that our bodies, though separated, remain aware

at the subatomic level. In that deeper ocean within. Shining
over the rolling waves of time. The way lovers do. And now—

I am the funeral ship that carries us both out to sea.
And yes, I remember the two of us in the 21st century rain

on the curb of a Manhattan sidewalk, our fingertips
touching, then braiding, our bodies entranced,

the two of us *seeing* each other in that moment,
the wild delight of it swirling within us, sweet, tantalizing,

the two of us kissing in the rain of that night, always now,
no matter the spinning of the planet into the gravitational pull

of the future, even after our bodies have long been given to the earth
and lifted into the winds encircling the globe, we hold each other

through the winters and springs and summers and falls
that others laugh and cry their way through, their bright voices

in the air around us fluttering in waves like the songs of birds
while the two of us, lovers new to one another, kiss.

Love rooted us.

           Together, exponential.

After, we spoke in tongues.

           Our fingers cupped the universe like water.

           —Ilyse Kusnetz

After reading, please view the film, *Clouds*, here—

To view a gallery of images, please use this link—

NOTES

The opening poem is from *Angel Bones* (Alice James Books, 2019) by Ilyse Kusnetz.

Anna Maria Island. Quoted passage is from Simon Makin's article ("Traveling" Brain Waves May be Critical for Cognition") in *Scientific American*, June 28, 2018.

Before/After. "Tollund, Grauballe, Nebelgard" is from section III of "The Tollund Man" by Seamus Heaney (*Wintering Out*, Faber & Faber, 1972).

Satellites. The epigraph is from "The Universe" by Gregory Alan Isakov (*The Weatherman*, Suitcase Town Music, 2013).

Heroes. Scientists Kohei Oda (Kyoto Institute of Technology) and Kenji Miyamoto (Keio University) led a team of researchers in the discovery of this bacterium in 2016.

Angioplasty. The italicized lyrics are from "Octopus's Garden." Words and music by Richard Starkey. Copyright © 1969. Startling Music Ltd. Copyright renewed. All rights administered by BMG Rights Management (US) LLC. All rights reserved. Used by Permission. Reprinted with permission of Hal Leonard LLC.

Cygnus the Swan. Many thanks to Simon Holbeche, an astronomer with Bath Astronomers, for assistance in calculating the distance between stars in this constellation.

Enewetak Atoll. I wish I'd followed up to ask Marshall more about his time in the Pacific, and the damage done to the places where he'd served and to those who have inhabited the islands for over a millennium. For example, from 1948-1958, the U.S. conducted 43 separate detonations—exploding more than 31 megatons of explosives. The first thermonuclear device ever tested at full scale, a hydrogen bomb that worked through nuclear fusion (nicknamed Ivy Mike) erased most of the island of Elugelab on the northern ring of the atoll, blasting a crater 160 feet deep and more than a mile wide. The levels of radioactivity at Enewetak—even to this day—are exponentially higher than those in the Chernobyl exclusion zone, or at Fukushima. Think: Plutonium-239, Plutonium-240. The latter has a half-life of 6,560 years. And the former? 24,100 years.

The Jurassic Coast. Here's an important source of information for us all: The International Union for Conservation of Nature's Red List of Threatened Species: https://www.iucnredlist.org

The Auditorium Cave. I'm so grateful for the research and help I received from Professor Giriraj Kumar, Professor of Rock Art Science and Indian Culture and founding Secretary General of the Rock Art Society of India. In discussing petroglyphs in the Auditorium Cave, Professor Giriraj tells me that he has studied the number of blows necessary to create similar cupules in quartzite rock. In 2002, Kumar supervised the replication of a cupule near Daraki-Chattan Cave over the course of two days—reaching a depth of 9.0 mm. That's slightly more than $1/3^{rd}$ of an inch. And to reach that depth, it took 28,327 strikes of stone on stone with deep concentration and dedication. For more, please see: Kumar, G. and Ram Krishna. 2014. "Understanding the technology of the Daraki-Chattan cupules: The cupule replication project." *Rock Art Research* 31 (2): 177-186. Melbourne.

Ashes, Ashes. In Australia, an Aboriginal Dreamtime story related to this piece is detailed in this article by Damon Cronshaw, "Burning Mountain at Wingen in the Upper Hunter has been burning for centuries." (*Newcastle Herald*, January 2, 2017).

Waiting for the Sun. For a detailed description of Canadian Wood Frogs, see "Biological Miracle" on the National Park Service website.

One Last Moment in the Vast City of Ants. For more information, please see Sally Schneider's "Concrete Poured Into Ant Colony Reveals Insect Megalopolis" in the March 15th, 2011 issue of *The Atlantic.* This poem is dedicated to Lewis Thomas.

Hyperion. The epigraph is from Robert Wrigley's poem, "The History of Gods" (*Anatomy of Melancholy and Other Poems*, Penguin Books, 2013). The last phrase, ". . . as we walked into the silence of the grove" is a nod to Sam Hamill's translation of Bashō's frog as it ". . . plunges into/ the sound of water" (*The Sound of Water: Haiku* by Bashō, Busan, Issa, and Other Poets, Shambhala, 2006).

Kissing in the Rain of New York. The epigraph is from Martin Craft's song, "Dragonfly" (Silver & Fire, 679, 2006).

The afterward couplets are from the poem, "Holding Albert Einstein's Hand," by Ilyse Kusnetz (*Small Hours,* Truman State University Press, 2014 and Alice James Books, 2021).

ACKNOWLEDGMENTS

I'm grateful to the editors for believing in this work and for publishing earlier versions of the following:

Dear Human at the Edge of Time (Paloma Press, Fall 2013). "Hyperion"
Terrain.org (Fall, 2022). "The Immortals," "Cuvier's Beaked Whales,"
"One Last Moment in the Vast City of Ants."
Red Canary Magazine (Summer, 2022). "Heroes."
The Massachusetts Review (Winter, 2021). "The Jurassic Coast."
Brevity (May, 2020). "Anna Maria Island" [*Did you know the common housefly…*].
The Georgia Review (Fall, 2017). "Ashes, Ashes."

★

I am *deeply* grateful to Carey Salerno for her belief in me and in the work I do, for her vision and guidance in this project from its earliest stages, and for her care in seeing each thing done right. Thank you to all at Alice James Books—both now and through the years—for your steadfast support of my work and for working so hard to see necessary voices take part in a larger poetic conversation now spanning fifty years. Many thanks to Julia Bouwsma for her fine-tuned attention to every word on the page. I'd also like to thank Anya Backlund at Blue Flower Arts for creating doorways into friendships and experiences that continually change my life for the better. And many thanks to Samar Hammam, at Rocking Chair Books, for that first phone call nearly twenty years ago, and for all the conversations since—your friendship and guidance (and wonderful eye in reading my manuscripts and offering advice) has seen me through the hardest of times.

As these manuscripts appeared, one draft to another, I leaned on the good hearts of these incredible writers and human beings with the hope that they might help the work in this trio of collections shine brighter—Donald Anderson, Laure-Anne Bosselaar, Nickole Brown, Stacey Lynn Brown, Corrinne Clegg Hales, Patrick Hicks, Lee Herrick, Arthur Kusnetz, Dunya Mikhail, June Sylvester Saraceno, and Christy Turner (who each read this work during the most trying of times). Thank you. Thank you. Thank you.

★

The album that accompanies this book (*Clouds*) was a collaborative project made possible by many kind-hearted souls and talented artists. I'm overwhelmed by the generosity of spirit each brought to the creation of this music, and I want to thank each for making an idea become a living artwork, a sound meditation that I hope will prove meaningful for you.

When listening to the album, you'll hear me singing and playing bass guitar, flugelhorn, acoustic guitar, living plants via PlantWave, a Resonant Garden, an Omnichord OM-84 (created by Arius Blaze and Ben Houston at Folktek), as well as an O-Coast synth from Make Noise.

This album would not have been possible without the phenomenal talent, knowledge, and work that Benjamin Kramer brought to every measure of the composition. Not only did he mix and master the album as the engineer, he played upright bass and piano, added string and horn arrangements, and much, much more.

You'll also hear vocalists Sarah Cossaboon and Chantal Thompson, great souls all.

Sunil Yapa added his own meditation of electric guitar and pedals, music that lifts the spirit.

Dan Veach added bass clarinet with a taste of mystery to it.

Úna ní Fhlannagáin added Harp to create a bridge of sound.

Fan Yang added piano and brought her signature joie de vivre to every note.

With tremendous thanks to the following choirs (which I recorded over several years):

...A large choir (maybe 80+ people) I recorded in 2022 during a reading at the Great Mother and New Father Conference in Nobleboro, Maine.

...The Kalakshetra Foundation in Chennai, India, where I was fortunate enough to record a chorus of about 80-120 students for this project. The birds are from the sacred banyan tree just outside of the hall where we recorded. Many thanks to poet Sonnet Mondal for organizing this trip and for always bringing people together.

...The school choir at Coláiste/Gaelcholáiste Choilm in Ballincollig, Ireland, including teachers Catherine Frost, Sean Lehane, Ronan Holohan, Carmel Falvey, Juliet Mullins, and Greta Costello, Principal Michelle Sliney, and (with much love to) Pádraigín O'Donoghue for organizing the recording and making it all possible. Thanks, also—to the Presentation Sisters at Nano Nagle Place in Cork—for allowing us to record in their beautiful chapel and for allowing me to live on the grounds there as I served as the inaugural John Montague International Poetry Fellow for the City of Cork in 2018, an annual post envisioned and founded by poet Patrick Cotter; I'll always be grateful to Pat for making a space for me in Ireland, especially at a time when I was so low, and needed to step away from the deep hollow at the center of my life. This fellowship helped me, in many ways, to begin to reengage with the world.

. . . an extraordinary panel at AWP ("From Verse to Stage and Screen: Veterans Adapt"), moderated by Peter Molin in 2017, with guest panelists Benjamin Busch, J.A. Moad, and Jenny Pacanowski. At one point, I asked all in the room to hum—and that recording is folded into *Clouds*.

Special thanks to J.A. Moad. You know why.

★

I send my love and gratitude to those mentioned above, and also to Tony Barnstone, Jefferson Beavers, Shannon Beets, Jeff Bell, Kevin Bowen, Seth Brady Tucker, Gayle Brandeis, Doyle Buhler, Camille Dungy, Pablo Cartaya, Matt Cashion, Sophie Cherry, Steven Church, Russell Conrad, Shawn Crouch, Roel Daamen, Rupa DasGupta, Rob Deemer, Kurt Erickson, Heidi Moss Erickson, Sarabjeet Garcha, Patsy Garoupa, Alison Granucci, Kelle Groom, Paul Guest, Nathalie Handal, Charles Hanzlicek, Lisa Lee Herrick, Faylita Hicks, Devin High, Garrett Hongo, T.R. Hummer, Ashwani Kumar, Dorianne Laux, Kwang Ho Lee, Rebecca Makkai, Tim Maxwell, Laura McCullough, Katie McDowell, Thomas McGuire, Christopher Merrill, Mujib Merhdad, Joe Millar, Sadek Mohammed, Peter Mountford, Soheil Najm, Matt O'Donnell, April Ossmann, Oliver de la Paz, Benjamin Percy, Susan Rich, Suzanne Roberts, Jake Runestad, John Schafer, Sean Sexton, Ravi Shankar, Jared Silvia, Krystal Sital, Patricia Smith, Michael Thomas, Chantal Thompson, Bill Tuell, Bruce Weigl, Sholeh Wolpé, Lidia Yuknavitch, and Arianne Zwartjes—thank you for allowing me to be a part of your phenomenal lives. One of my deep regrets is in not adequately expressing how grateful I am to each of you.

To Corrinne Clegg Hales—I was the shy kid at the back of the class with the profound stammer, and I'll always be grateful for your encouragement and for all that you taught me about the art itself. Thank you for your friendship and mentorship over the years, Connie.

To Patrick Hicks—With every draft and revision, you've been there as my first reader. It's been an unspoken thing, a gift of such profound magnitude, and always with a keen eye to the art itself, while—at a deeper level—helping me as I attempt to write my way into the rest of my life.

To Stacey Lynn Brown—Through the highs and lows the years and decades bring, you remain a constant friend through it all. It's been a gift to be a part of your life. Just know—if you find yourself in a bar fight (which I don't recommend), don't worry, I got your back.

To Benjamin Busch—Thanks for keeping me upright and steady in the low times, man, and for hitting the high notes that remind us all that Rock is not dead.

To June Sylvester Saraceno—Thanks for being the gift of a sister I met late in a life. I'll meet you at the river with Luna and Dene. Thank you for always being there for me.

I send my abiding love to friends and family, loved ones all, both near and far.

★

Dear Reader, you hold in your hands a book that I wish I didn't have to write. I know that for many of you it will evoke memories from your own lives, or the experiences of those you love. I wish you well in your journey, and I hope the meditations in this trio of books prove meaningful as you navigate the landscape of love and loss. If you choose to lean into projects that aim to fight cancer, or those that might help those battling the disease, or survivors who have lost loved ones, please contact me through the publisher or my agents if you believe I might be able to help with your good work. Of course, this book is both incredibly specific in its meditation on loss—and also global in its intent. If you're working on a project to help the planet, in terms of climate change and species extinction, please reach out to me and let me know if I can be of help.

*

Ilyse, a small amount of ash hangs in a silver locket around my neck. You listen to my heartbeat through the wall of my chest, hear each breath resonating in the bones of my sternum, feel the heat of blood radiating from my skin.

Every word I speak rises through you before finding its way into the world.

RECENT TITLES FROM ALICE JAMES BOOKS

I Am the Most Dangerous Thing, Candace Williams

Burning Like Her Own Planet, Vandana Khanna

Standing in the Forest of Being Alive, Katie Farris

Feast, Ina Cariño

Decade of the Brain: Poems, Janine Joseph

American Treasure, Jill McDonough

We Borrowed Gentleness, J. Estanislao Lopez

Brother Sleep, Aldo Amparán

Sugar Work, Katie Marya

Museum of Objects Burned by the Souls in Purgatory, Jeffrey Thomson

Constellation Route, Matthew Olzmann

How to Not Be Afraid of Everything, Jane Wong

Brocken Spectre, Jacques J. Rancourt

No Ruined Stone, Shara McCallum

The Vault, Andrés Cerpa

White Campion, Donald Revell

Last Days, Tamiko Beyer

If This Is the Age We End Discovery, Rosebud Ben-Oni

Pretty Tripwire, Alessandra Lynch

Inheritance, Taylor Johnson

The Voice of Sheila Chandra, Kazim Ali

Arrow, Sumita Chakraborty

Country, Living, Ira Sadoff

Hot with the Bad Things, Lucia LoTempio

Witch, Philip Matthews

Neck of the Woods, Amy Woolard

Little Envelope of Earth Conditions, Cori A. Winrock

Alice James Books is committed to publishing books that matter. The press was founded in 1973 in Boston, Massachusetts to give women access to publishing. As a cooperative, authors performed the day-to-day undertakings of the press. The press continues to expand and grow from its formative roots, guided by its founding values of access, excellence, inclusivity, and collaboration in publishing. Its mission is to publish books that matter and preserve a place of belonging for poets who inspire us. AJB seeks to broaden our collective interpretation of what constitutes the American poetic voice and is dedicated to helping its artists achieve purposeful engagement with broad audiences and communities nationwide. The press was named for Alice James, sister to William and Henry, whose extraordinary gift for writing went unrecognized during her lifetime.

Designed by Alban Fischer

Printed by Sheridan Saline